THE MARBLE PROPHECY.

THE MARBLE PROPHECY,

AND OTHER POEMS.

BY

J. G. HOLLAND,

AUTHOR OF "BITTER SWEET," "KATHRINA," ETC., ETC.

NEW YORK:
SCRIBNER, ARMSTRONG & CO.
1872.

CONTENTS.

THE MARBLE PROPHECY.

The harlequins are out in force to-day—
The piebald Swiss—and in the vestibule
Of great St. Peter's rings the rhythmic tread
Of Roman nobles, uniformed and armed
As the Pope's Guard; and while their double
line
With faultless curve enters the open door,
And sways and sparkles up the splendid
nave,
Between the walls of humbler soldiery,
And parts to pass the altar—keeping step
To the proud beating of their Roman
hearts—
A breeze of whispered admiration sweeps
The crowds that gaze, and dics within the
dome.

St. Peter's toe (the stump of it) was cold
An hour ago, but waxes warm apace
With rub of handkerchiefs, and dainty touch
Of lips and foreheads.

Smug behind their screen
Sit the Pope's Choir. No woman enters there;
For woman is impure, and makes impure
By voice and presence! Mary, mother of God!
Not thy own sex may sing thee in the courts
Of The All-Holy!—Only man, pure man!
Doubt not the purity of some of these—
Angels before their time—nor doubt
That they will sing like angels, when Papa,
Borne on the shoulders of his stalwart men
(The master rode an ass), and canopied
By golden tapestries—the triple crown

Upon his brow, the nodding peacock plumes
Far heralding his way—shall come to take
His incense and his homage.

I will go.
'Tis a brave pageant, to be seen just once.
'Tis a brave pageant, but one does not like
To smutch his trousers kneeling to a man,
Or bide the stare that follows if he fail;
So, having seen it once, one needs not wait.

What is the feast? Let's see: ah! I recall:
St. Peter's chair was brought from Antioch
So many years ago;—the worse for wear
No doubt, and never quite luxurious,

But valued as a piece of furniture
By Rome above all price; and so they give
High honor to the anniversary.
'Tis well; in Rome they make account of chairs.
If less in heaven, it possibly may be
Because they're greatly occupied by joy
Over bad men made penitent and pure
By this same chair! Who knows?

I'll to the door!
The sun seems kind and simple in the sky
After such pomp. I thank thee, Sun! Thou hast
A smile like God, that reaches to the heart
Direct and sweet, without the ministries
Of scene and ceremonial! Thy rays
Fall not in benediction at the ends

Of two pale fingers; but thy warmth and
    light
Wrap well the cold dark world. I need
    no prism
To teach my soul that thou art beautiful:
It would divide thee, and confuse my sight.
Shine freely, sun! No mighty mother
    church
Stands mediator between thee and me!
Ay, shine on these—all these in shivering
    need—
To whom God's precious love is doled or
    sold
By sacerdotal hucksters! Shine on these,
And teach them that the God of Life
    and Light
Dwells not alone in temples made by
    hands;
And that the path to Him, from every
    soul,
In every farthest corner of the earth,
Is as direct as are thy rays to thee!

Ha! Pardon! Have I hurt you? Wella-
day!
I was not looking for a beggar here:—
Indeed, was looking upward! But I see
You're here by royal license—with a badge
Made of good brass. Come nearer to me!
there:
Take double alms, and give me chance to
read
The number on your breast. So: "Sev-
enty-seven"!
'Tis a good number, man, and quite at
home
About the temple. Well, you have hard
fare,
But many brothers and no end of shows!
Think it not ill that they will spend to-
day,
Touching this chair, enough of time and
gold
To gorge the poor of Rome. The men
who hold

The church in charge—who are, indeed,
 the church—
Have little time to give to starving men.
Be thankful for your label! Only one
Can be the beggar "Number seventy-
 seven"!
They are distinguished persons: so are you!
You must be patient, though it seems, I
 grant,
A trifle odd that when a miracle
Is wrought before you, it will never take
A useful turn, as in the olden time,
And give you loaves and fishes, or in-
 crease
Your little dinners!

Still the expectant crowds
Press up the street from round St. Angelo,
And thread the circling colonnade, or cross
With hurried steps the broad piazza—
 crowds

That pass the portal, and at once are lost
Within the vaulted glooms, as morning mist
Is quenched by morning air.

It is God's house—
The noblest temple ever reared to Him
By hands of men—the culminating deed
Of a great church—the topmost reach of
art
For the enshrinement of the Christian faith
In sign and symbol. Holiness becomes
The temple of the Holy!

And these crowds?
Come they to pour the worship of their
hearts
Like wine upon the altar? Who are they?
Last night, we hear, the theatre was full.
It was a spectacle: they went to see.

All yesterday they thronged the galleries,
Or roved among the ruins, or drove out
Upon the broad campagna—just to see.
This afternoon, with gaudy equipage,
(Their Bædeker and Murray left at home),
They'll be upon the Pincio—to see.
And so this morning, learning of the chair
And the Pope's coming, they are here to see
(The men in swallow-tails, their wives in
black),
The grandest spectacle of all the week.
Make way ye men of poverty and dirt
Who fringe the outer lines! Make open-
way
And let them pass! This is the House of
God,
And swallow-tails are of fine moment here!

The ceremony has begun within.
I hear the far, faint voices of the choir,

As if a door in heaven were left ajar,
And cherubim were singing . . . Now I hear
The sharp, metallic chink of grounded arms
Upon the marble, as His Holiness
Moves up the lines of bristling bayonets
That guard his progress. . . . But I stay
 alone.
Nay, I will to the Vatican, and there,
In converse with the thoughts of manlier
 men,
Pass the great morning! I shall be alone—
Ay, all alone with thee, Laocöon!

"A feast day and no entrance"? Can
 one's gold
Unloose a soul from purgatorial bonds
And ope the gates of heaven, without the
 power
To draw a bolt at the Museum? Wait!

Laocöon! thou great embodiment
Of human life and human history!
Thou record of the past, thou prophecy
Of the sad future, thou majestic voice,
Pealing along the ages from old time!
Thou wail of agonized humanity!
There lives no thought in marble like to
thee!
Thou hast no kindred in the Vatican,
But standest separate among the dreams
Of old mythologies—alone—alone!
The beautiful Apollo at thy side
Is but a marble dream, and dreams are all
The gods and goddesses and fauns and fates
That populate these wondrous halls; but
thou,
Standing among them, liftest up thyself
In majesty of meaning, till they sink
Far from the sight, no more significant
Than the poor toys of children. For thou
art
A voice from out the world's experience,

Speaking of all the generations past
To all the generations yet to come
Of the long struggle, the sublime despair,
The wild and weary agony of man!

Ay, Adam and his offspring, in the toils
Of the twin serpents Sin and Suffering,
Thou dost impersonate; and as I gaze
Upon the twining monsters that enfold
In unrelaxing, unrelenting coils,
Thy awful energies, and plant their fangs
Deep in thy quivering flesh, while still thy might
In fierce convulsion foils the fateful wrench
That would destroy thee, I am overwhelmed
With a strange sympathy of kindred pain,
And see through gathering tears the tragedy,
The curse and conflict of a ruined race!

Those Rhodian sculptors were gigantic men,
Whose inspirations came from other source
Than their religion, though they chose to
speak
Through its familiar language,—men who
saw,
And, seeing quite divinely, felt how weak
To cure the world's great woe were all
the powers
Whose reign their age acknowledged. So
they sat—
The immortal three—and pondered long and
well
What one great work should speak the
truth for them,—
What one great work should rise and testify
That they had found the topmost fact of
life,
Above the reach of all philosophies
And all religions—every scheme of man
To placate or dethrone. That fact they
found,

And moulded into form. The silly priest
Whose desecrations of the altar stirred
The vengeance of his God, and summoned forth
The wreathed gorgons of the slimy deep
To crush him and his children, was the word
By which they spoke to their own age and race,
That listened and applauded, knowing not
That high above the small significance
They apprehended, rose the grand intent
That mourned their doom and breathed a world's despair!

Be sure it was no fable that inspired
So grand an utterance. Perchance some leaf
From an old Hebrew record had conveyed
A knowledge of the genesis of man.
Perchance some fine conception rose in them
Of unity of nature and of race,

Springing from one beginning. Nay, perchance
Some vision flashed before their thoughtful eyes
Inspired by God, which showed the mighty man,
Who, unbegotten, had begot a race
That to his lot was linked through countless time
By living chains, from which in vain it strove
To wrest its tortured limbs and leap amain
To freedom and to rest! It matters not:
The double word—the fable and the fact,
The childish figment and the mighty truth,
Are blent in one. The first was for a day
And dying Rome; the last for later time
And all mankind.

These sculptors spoke their word
And then they died; and Rome—imperial Rome—

The mistress of the world—debauched by
blood
And foul with harlotries—fell prone at length
Among the trophies of her crimes and slept.
Down toppling one by one her helpless gods
Fell to the earth, and hid their shattered
forms
Within the dust that bore them, and among
The ruined shrines and crumbling masonry
Of their old temples. Still this wondrous
group,
From its long home upon the Esquiline,
Beheld the centuries of change, and stood,
Impersonating in its conscious stone
The unavailing struggle to crowd back
The closing folds of doom. It paused to
hear
A strange New Name proclaimed among
the streets,
And catch the dying shrieks of martyred
men,
And see the light of hope and heroism

Kindling in many eyes; and then it fell;
And in the ashes of an empire swathed
Its aching sense, and hid its tortured forms.

The old life went, the new life came; and Rome
That slew the prophets built their sepulchres,
And filled her heathen temples with the shrines
Of Christian saints whom she had tossed to beasts,
Or crucified, or left to die in chains
Within her dungeons. Ay, the old life went
But came again. The primitive, true age—
The simple, earnest age—when Jesus Christ
The Crucified was only known and preached,
Struck hands with paganism and passed away.

Rome built new temples and installed new
names;
Set up her graven images, and gave
To Pope and priests the keeping of her gods.
Again she grasped at power no longer hers
By right of Roman prowess, and stretched
out
Her hand upon the consciences of men.
The godlike liberty with which the Christ
Had made his people free she stole from them,
And bound them slaves to new observances.
Her times, her days, her ceremonials
Imposed a burden grievous to be borne,
And millions groaned beneath it. Nay, she
grew
The vengeful persecutor of the free
Who would not bear her yoke, and bathed
her hands
In blood as sweet as ever burst from hearts
Torn from the bosoms of the early saints
Within her Coliseum. She assumed
To be the arbiter of destiny.

Those whom she bound or loosed upon the
earth,
Were bound or loosed in heaven! In God's
own place,
She sat as God—supreme, infallible!
She shut the door of knowledge to man-
kind,
And bound the Word Divine. She sucked
the juice
Of all prosperities within her realms,
Until her gaudy temples blazed with gold,
And from a thousand altars flashed the fire
Of priceless gems. To win her countless
wealth
She sold as merchandise the gift of God.
She took the burden which the cross had
borne,
And bound it fast to scourged and writh-
ing loins
In thriftless Penance, till her devotees
Fled from their kind to find the boon of
peace,

And died in banishment. Beneath her sway,
The proud old Roman blood grew thin and
mean
Till virtue was the name it gave to fear,
Till heroism and brigandage were one,
And neither slaves nor beggars knew their
shame!

What marvel that a shadow fell, world-wide,
And brooded o'er the ages? Was it strange
That in those dim and drowsy centuries,
When the dumb earth had ceased to quake
beneath
The sounding wheels of progress, and the
life
That erst had flamed so high had sunk so
low
In cold monastic glooms and forms as cold,
The buried gods should listen in their sleep
And dream of resurrection? Was it strange

That listening well they should at length
awake,
And struggle from their pillows? Was it
strange
That men whose vision grovelled should
perceive
The dust in motion, and with rapture greet
Each ancient deity with loud acclaim,
As if he brought with him the good old
days
Of manly art and poetry and power?
Nay, was it strange that as they raised them-
selves,
And cleaned their drowsy eyelids of the dust,
And took their godlike attitudes again,
The grand old forms should feel themselves
at home—
Saving perhaps a painful sense that men
Had dwindled somewhat? Was it strange,
at last,
That all these gods should be installed anew,
And share the palace with His Holiness,

And that the Pope and Christian Rome can
show
No art that equals that which had its birth
In pagan inspiration? Ah, what shame!
That after two millenniums of Christ,
Rome calls to her the thirsty tribes of earth,
And smites the heathen marble with her rod,
And bids them drink the best she has to
give!

And when the gods were on their feet again
It was thy time to rise, Laocöon!
Those Rhodian sculptors had foreseen it all.
Their word was true: thou hadst the right
to live.

In the quick sunlight on the Esquiline,
Where thou didst sleep, De Fredis kept his
vines;

And long above thee grew the grapes whose
blood
Ran wild in Christian arteries, and fed
The fire of Christian revels. Ah what fruit
Sucked up the marrow of thy marble there!
What fierce, mad dreams were those that
scared the souls
Of men who drank, nor guessed what ichor
stung
Their crimson lips, and tingled in their veins!
Strange growths were those that sprang
above thy sleep:
Vines that were serpents; huge and ugly
trunks
That took the forms of human agony—
Contorted, gnarled and grim—and leaves
that bore
The semblance of a thousand tortured hands,
And snaky tendrils that entwined them-
selves
Around all forms of life within their reach,
And crushed or blighted them!

At last the spade
Slid down to find the secret of the vines,
And touched thee with a thrill that startled
Rome,
And swiftly called a shouting multitude
To witness thy unveiling.

Ah what joy
Greeted the rising from thy long repose!
And one, the mighty master of his time,
The king of Christian art, with strong,
sad face
Looked on, and wondered with the giddy
crowd,—
Looked on and learned (too late, alas! for
him),
That his humanity and God's own truth
Were more than Christian Rome, and spoke
in words
Of larger import. Humbled Angelo
Bowed to the masters of the early days,

Grasped their strong hands across the
centuries,
And went his way despairing!

Thou, meantime,
Dids't find thyself installed among the gods
Here in the Vatican; and thou, to-day,
Hast the same word for those who read thee
well
As when thou wast created. Rome has
failed:
Humanity is writhing in the toils
Of the old monsters as it writhed of old,
And there is neither help nor hope in her.
Her priests, her shrines, her rites, her
mummeries,
Her pictures and her pageants, are as weak
To break the hold of Sin and Suffering
As those her reign displaced. Her iron
hand

Shrivels the manhood it presumes to bless,
Drives to disgust or infidelity
The strong and free who dare to think and
judge,
And wins a kiss from coward lips alone.
She does not preach the Gospel to the poor,
But takes it from their hands. The men
who tread
The footsteps of the Master, and bow down
Alone to Him, she brands as heretics
Or hunts as fiends. She drives beyond her
gates
The Christian worshippers of other climes,
And other folds and faiths, as if their brows
Were white with leprosy, and grants them
there
With haughty scorn the privilege to kneel
In humble worship of the common Lord!

Is this the Christ, or look we still for Him?
Is the old problem solved, or lingers yet

The grand solution? Ay Laocöon!
Thy word is true, for Christian Rome has failed,
And I behold humanity in thee
As those who shaped thee saw it, when old Rome
In that far pagan evening fell asleep.

THE WINGS.

A feeble wail was heard at night,
  And a stifled cry of joy;
And when the morn broke cool and light,
They bore to the mother's tearful sight
  A fair and lovely boy.

Months passed away;
And day by day
  The mother hung about her child
As in his little cot he lay,
  And watched him as he smiled,
And threw his hands into the air,
  And turned above his large, bright eyes,
With an expression half of prayer
And half of strange surprise;
    For hovering o'er his downy head

A dainty vision hung.
  Fluttering, swaying,
Unsteadily it swung,
    As if suspended by a thread,
  His own sweet breath obeying.

Sometimes with look of wild beseeching
  He marked it as it dropped
Almost within his awkward reaching,
And as the vision stopped
  Beyond his anxious grasp,
  And cheated the quick clasp
Of dimpled hands, and quite
Smothered his chirrup of delight,
  And he saw his effort vain
  And the bright vision there again
Dancing before his sight,
    His eyes grew dim with tears,
    Till o'er the flooded spheres
      The soothing eye-lids crept,
      And the tired infant slept.

He saw—his mother could not see—
A presence and a mystery:
    Two waving wings,
Spangled with silver, starlike things:
    No form of light was borne between;
      Only the wings were seen!

Years steal away with silent feet,
  And he, the little one,
With brow more fair and voice more sweet
  Is playing in the sun.
Flowers are around him and the songs
  Of bounding streams and happy birds,
But sweeter than their sweetest tongues
  Break forth his own glad words.
          And as he sings
          The wings, the wings!
        Before him still they fly!
  And nothing that the summer brings
        Can so entice his eye.
      Hovering here, hovering there,
          Hovering everywhere,

They flash and shine among the flowers,
While dripping sheen in golden showers
Falls through the air where'er they hover
Upon the radiant things they cover.
Hurrying here, hurrying there,
Hurrying everywhere,
He plucks the flowers they shine upon,
But while he plucks their light is gone!
And casting down the faded things,
Onward he springs
To follow the wings!

Years run away with silent feet;
The boy, to manhood grown,
Within a shadowy retreat
Stands anxious and alone.
His bosom heaves with heavy sighs,
His hair hangs damp and long,
But fiery purpose fills his eyes,
And his limbs are large and strong:
And there above a gentle hill,

The wings are hovering still,
While their soft radiance, rich and warm,
Falls on a maiden's form.

And see! again he starts,
And onward darts,
Then pauses with a fierce and sudden pain,
Then presses on again,
Till with mixed thoughts of rapture and despair,
He kneels before her there:—
With hands together prest,
He prays to her with low and passionate calls,
And, like a snow-flake pure, she flutters, falls,
And melts upon his breast.

Long in that dearest trance he hung—
Then raised, his eyes; the wings that swung
In glancing circles round his head

Afar had fled,
And wheeled, with calm and graceful flight,
Over a scene
That glowed with glories beauteously bright
Beneath their sheen.

High in the midst a monument arose,
Of pale enduring marble; calm and still,
It seemed a statue of sublime repose,
The silent speaker of a mighty will.

Its sides were hung around
With boughs of evergreen; and its long shaft was crowned
With a bright laurel-wreath,
And glittering beneath
Were piled great heaps of gold upon the ground.
Children were playing near—fair boys and girls,

Who shook their sunny curls,
And laughed and sang in mirthfulness of spirit,
And in their childish pleasures
Danced around the treasures
Of gold and honor they were to inherit.

The sight has fired his brain;
Onward he springs again.
O'er ruined blocks
Of wild and perilous rocks,
Through long damp caves, o'er pitfalls dire,
And maddening scenes of blood and fire,
Fainting with heat,
Benumbed with cold,
With weary, aching feet,
He sternly toils, and presses on to greet
The monument, the laurels and the gold.

Years have passed by; a shattered form
Leans faintly on a monument;
His glazing eyes are bent
In sadness down: a tear falls to the ground
That through the furrows of his cheek hath
wound.
The children beautiful have ceased to play,
Tarnished the marble stands with dark
decay,
The laurels all are dead, and flown the gold
away

Once more he raised his eyes; before
him lay
A dim and lonely vale,
And feebly tottering in the downward
way
Walked spectres cold and pale.
And darkling groves of shadowy cypress
sprung

Among the damp clouds that around them
hung.
One vision only cheers his aching sight;
Those wings of light
Have lost their varied hues, and changed to
white,
And, with a gentle motion, slowly wave
Over a new made grave.
He casts one faltering, farewell look behind,
Around, above, one mournful glance he
throws,
Then with a cheerful smile, and trusting
mind,
Moves feebly toward the valley of repose.
He stands above the grave; dull shudders
creep
Along his limbs, cold drops are on his brow;
One sigh he heaves, and sinking into sleep
He drops and disappears;—and dropping
now,
The wings have followed too.
But, lo! new visions burst upon the view!

They reappear in glory bright and new!
And to their sweet embrace a soul is given,
And on the wings of HOPE an angel flies
to HEAVEN.

INTIMATIONS.

WHAT glory then! What darkness now!
  A glimpse, a thrill, and it is flown!
  I reach, I grasp, but stand alone,
With empty arms and upward brow!

Ye may not see, O weary eyes!
  The band of angels, swift and bright,
  That pass, but cannot wake your sight,
Down trooping from the crowded skies.

O heavy ears! Ye may not hear
  The strains that pass my conscious soul,
  And seek, but find no earthly goal,
Far falling from another sphere.

Ah! soul of mine! Ah! soul of mine!
  Thy sluggish senses are but bars
  That stand between thee and the stars,
And shut thee from the world divine.

For something sweeter far than sound,
  And something finer than the light
  Comes through the discord and the night
And penetrates, or wraps thee round.

Nay, God is here, couldst thou but see;
  All things of beauty are of Him;
  And heaven, that holds the cherubim,
As lovingly embraces thee!

If thou hast apprehended well
  The tender glory of a flower,
  Which moved thee, by some subtle power
Whose source and sway thou couldst not tell;

If thou hast kindled to the sweep
Of stormy clouds across the sky,
Or gazed with tranced and tearful eye,
And swelling breast, upon the deep;

If thou hast felt the throb and thrill
Of early day and happy birds,
While peace, that drowned thy chosen words
Has flowed from thee in glad good-will,

Then hast thou drunk the heavenly dew;
Then have thy feet in rapture trod
The pathway of a thought of God;
And death can show thee nothing new.

For heaven and beauty are the same,—
Of God the all-informing thought,
To sweet, supreme expression wrought,
And syllabled by sound and flame.

The light that beams from childhood's eyes,
  The charm that dwells in summer woods,
  The holy influence that broods
O'er all things under twilight skies,—

The music of the simple notes
  That rise from happy human homes,
  The joy in life of all that roams
Upon the earth, and all that floats,

Proclaim that heaven's sweet providence
  Enwraps the homely earth in whole,
  And finds the secret of the soul
Through channels subtler than the sense.

O soul of mine! Throw wide thy door,
  And cleanse thy paths from doubt and sin;
  And the bright flood shall enter in
And give thee heaven forevermore!

WORDS.

The robin repeats his two musical words,
  The meadow-lark whistles his one refrain;
  And steadily, over and over again,
The same song swells from a hundred birds.

Bobolink, chickadee, blackbird and jay,
  Thrasher and woodpecker, cuckoo and
      wren,
  Each sings its word, or its phrase, and then
It has nothing further to sing or to say.

Into that word, or that sweet little phrase,
  All there may be of its life must crowd;
  And lulling and liquid, or hoarse and loud,
It breathes out its burden of joy and praise.

A little child sits in his father's door,
Chatting and singing with careless tongue;
A thousand beautiful words are sung,
And he holds unuttered a thousand more.

Words measure power; and they measure thine;
Greater art thou in thy prattling moods
Than all the singers of all the woods;
They are brutes only, but thou art divine.

Words measure destiny. Power to declare
Infinite ranges of passion and thought
Holds with the infinite only its lot,—
Is of eternity only the heir.

Words measure life, and they measure its joy!
Thou hast more joy in thy childish years
Than the birds of a hundred tuneful spheres,
So—sing with the beautiful birds, my boy!

SLEEPING AND DREAMING.

I softly sink into the bath of sleep:
  With eyelids shut, I see around me close
The mottled, violet vapors of the deep,
  That wraps me in repose.

I float all night in the ethereal sea
  That drowns my pain and weariness in
      balm,
Careless of where its currents carry me,
  Or settle into calm.

That which the ear can hear is silent all;
  But, in the lower stillness which I reach,
Soft whispers call me, like the distant fall
  Of waves upon the beach.

Now like the mother who with patient care
Has soothed to rest her faint, o'erwearied boy,
My spirit leaves the couch, and seeks the air
For freedom and for joy.

Drunk up like vapors by the morning sun
The past and future rise and disappear;
And times and spaces gather home, and run
Into a common sphere.

My youth is round me, and the silent tomb
Has burst to set its fairest prisoner free,
And I await her in the dewy gloom
Of the old trysting tree.

I mark the flutter of her snowy dress,
I hear the tripping of her fairy feet,
And now, pressed closely in a pure caress,
With ardent joy we meet.

I tell again the story of my love,
  I drink again her lip's delicious wine,
And, while the same old stars look down above,
  Her eyes look up to mine.

I dream that I am dreaming, and I start;
  Then dream that nought so real comes in dreams;
Then kiss again to reassure my heart
  That she is what she seems.

Our steps tend homeward. Lingering at the gate,
  I breathe, and breathe again, my fond good night.
She shuts the cruel door, and still I wait
  To watch her window-light.

I see the shadow of her dainty head,
On curtains that I pray her hand may stir,
Till all is dark; and then I seek my bed
To dream I dream of her.

Like the swift moon that slides from cloud to cloud,
With only hurried space to smile between,
I pierce the phantoms that around me crowd,
And glide from scene to scene.

I clasp warm hands that long have lain in dust,
I hear sweet voices that have long been still,
And earth and sea give up their hallowed trust
In answer to my will.

And now, high-gazing toward the starry
dome,
I see three airy forms come floating
down—
The long-lost angels of my early home—
My night of joy to crown.

They pause above, beyond my eager
reach,
With arms enwreathed and forms of heav-
enly grace;
And smiling back the love that smiles from
each,
I see them, face to face.

They breathe no language, but their holy
eyes
Beam an embodied blessing on my heart,
That warm within my trustful bosom
lies,
And never will depart.

I drink the effluence, till through all my soul
  I feel a flood of peaceful rapture flow,
That swells to joy at last, and bursts control,
  And I awake; but lo!

With eyelids shut, I hold the vision fast,
  And still detain it by my ardent prayer,
Till faint and fainter grown, it fades at last
  Into the silent air.

My God! I thank Thee for the bath of sleep,
  That wraps in balm my weary heart and
      brain,
And drowns within its waters still and deep
  My sorrow and my pain.

I thank Thee for my dreams, which loose
      the bond
  That binds my spirit to its daily load,
And give it angel wings, to fly beyond
  Its slumber-bound abode.

4

I thank Thee for these glimpses of the clime
  That lies beyond the boundaries of sense,
Where I shall wash away the stains of time
  In floods of recompense:—

Where, when this body sleeps to wake no
    more,
  My soul shall rise to everlasting dreams,
And find unreal all it saw before
  And real all that seems.

ON THE RIGHI.

ON the Righi Kulm we stood,
  Lovely Floribel and I,
While the morning's crimson flood
  Streamed along the eastern sky.
Reddened every mountain peak
  Into rose, from twilight dun;
But the blush upon her cheek
  Was not lighted by the sun!

On the Righi Kulm we sat,
  Lovely Floribel and I,
Plucking blue-bells for her hat
  From a mound that blossomed nigh.
"We are near to heaven," she sighed,
  While her raven lashes fell.
"Nearer," softly I replied,
  "Than the mountain's height may tell."

Down the Righi's side we sped,
  Lovely Floribel and I,
But her morning blush had fled,
  And the blue-bells all were dry.
Of the height the dream was born;
  Of the lower air it died;
And the passion of the morn
  Flagged and fell at eventide.

From the breast of blue Lucerne,
  Lovely Floribel and I
Saw the brand of sunset burn
  On the Righi Kulm, and die.
And we wondered, gazing thus,
  If our dream would still remain
On the height, and wait for us
  Till we climb to heaven again!

GRADATIM.

HEAVEN is not reached at a single bound,
  But we build the ladder by which we rise
  From the lowly earth to the vaulted skies,
And we mount to its summit round by
      round.

I count this thing to be grandly true:
  That a noble deed is a step toward God,—
  Lifting the soul from the common clod
To a purer air and a broader view.

We rise by the things that are under feet;
  By what we have mastered of good and
      gain;
  By the pride deposed and the passion slain,
And the vanquished ills that we hourly
      meet.

We hope, we aspire, we resolve, we trust,
When the morning calls us to life and light,
But our hearts grow weary, and, ere the night,
Our lives are trailing the sordid dust.

We hope, we resolve, we aspire, we pray,
And we think that we mount the air on wings
Beyond the recall of sensual things,
While our feet still cling to the heavy clay.

Wings for the angels, but feet for men!
We may borrow the wings to find the way—
We may hope, and resolve, and aspire, and pray;
But our feet must rise, or we fall again.

Only in dreams is a ladder thrown
From the weary earth to the sapphire walls;
But the dreams depart, and the vision falls,
And the sleeper wakes on his pillow of stone.

Heaven is not reached at a single bound;
But we build the ladder by which we rise
From the lowly earth to the vaulted skies,
And we mount to its summit, round by round.

RETURNING CLOUDS.

THE clouds are returning after the rain.
All the long morning they steadily sweep
From the blue Northwest, o'er the upper main,
In a peaceful flight to their Eastern sleep.

With sails that the cool wind fills or furls,
And shadows that darken the billowy grass,
Freighted with amber or piled with pearls,
Fleets of fair argosies rise and pass.

The earth smiles back to the smiling throng
From greening pasture and blooming field,

For the earth that had sickened with thirst
so long
Has been touched by the hand of The
Rain, and healed.

The old man sits 'neath the tall elm trees,
And watches the pageant with dreamy
eyes,
While his white locks stir to the same cool
breeze
That scatters the silver along the skies.

The old man's eyelids are wet with tears—
Tears of sweet pleasure and sweeter
pain—
For his thoughts are driving back over the
years
In beautiful clouds after life's long rain.

Sorrows that drowned all the springs of his life,
Trials that crushed him with pitiless beat,
Storms of temptation and tempests of strife,
Float o'er his memory tranquil and sweet.

And the old man's spirit, made soft and bright
By the long, long rain that had bent him low,
Sees a vision of angels on wings of white,
In the trooping clouds as they come and go.

EUREKA.

WHOM I crown with love is royal;
  Matters not her blood or birth;
She is queen, and I am loyal
  To the noblest of the earth.

Neither place, nor wealth, nor title,
  Lacks the man my friendship owns;
His distinction, true and vital,
  Shines supreme o'er crowns and thrones.

Where true love bestows its sweetness,
  Where true friendship lays its hand,
Dwells all greatness, all completeness,
  All the wealth of every land.

Man is greater than condition,
  And where man himself bestows,
He begets, and gives position
  To the gentlest that he knows.

Neither miracle nor fable
  Is the water changed to wine;
Lords and ladies at my table
  Prove Love's simplest fare divine.

And if these accept my duty,
  If the loved my homage own,
I have won all worth and beauty;
  I have found the magic stone.

WHERE SHALL THE BABY'S DIMPLE BE?

OVER the cradle the mother hung,
  Softly crooning a slumber-song;
And these were the simple words she sung
  All the evening long:

"Cheek or chin, or knuckle or knee,
Where shall the baby's dimple be?
Where shall the angel's finger rest
When he comes down to the baby's nest?
Where shall the angel's touch remain
When he awakens my babe again?"

Still as she bent and sang so low,
  A murmur into her music broke;
And she paused to hear, for she could but
    know
  The baby's angel spoke.

"Cheek or chin, or knuckle or knee,
Where shall the baby's dimple be?
Where shall my finger fall and rest
When I come down to the baby's nest?
Where shall my finger's touch remain
When I awaken your babe again?"

Silent the mother sat, and dwelt
  Long in the sweet delay of choice;
And then by her baby's side she knelt,
  And sang with pleasant voice:

"Not on the limb, O angel dear!
For the charm with its youth will disappear;
Not on the cheek shall the dimple be,
For the harboring smile will fade and flee;
But touch thou the chin with an impress
    deep,
And my baby the angel's seal shall keep."

THE HEART OF THE WAR.

(1864.)

PEACE in the clover-scented air,
  And stars within the dome;
And underneath, in dim repose,
  A plain, New England home.
Within, a murmur of low tones
  And sighs from hearts oppressed,
Merging in prayer, at last, that brings
  The balm of silent rest.

I've closed a hard day's work, Marty,—
  The evening chores are done;
And you are weary with the house,
  And with the little one.
But he is sleeping sweetly now,
  With all our pretty brood;
So come and sit upon my knee,
  And it will do me good.

Oh, Marty! I must tell you all
  The trouble in my heart,
And you must do the best you can
  To take and bear your part.
You've seen the shadow on my face;
  You've felt it day and night;
For it has filled our little home,
  And banished all its light.

I did not mean it should be so,
  And yet I might have known
That hearts which live as close as ours
  Can never keep their own.
But we are fallen on evil times,
  And, do whate'er I may,
My heart grows sad about the war,
  And sadder every day.

I think about it when I work,
  And when I try to rest,

And never more than when your head
  Is pillowed on my breast;
For then I see the camp-fires blaze,
  And sleeping men around,
Who turn their faces toward their homes,
  And dream upon the ground.

I think about the dear, brave boys,
  My mates in other years,
Who pine for home and those they love,
  Till I am choked with tears.
With shouts and cheers they marched away
  On glory's shining track,
But, Ah! how long, how long they stay!
  How few of them come back!

One sleeps beside the Tennessee,
  And one beside the James,
And one fought on a gallant ship
  And perished in its flames.

And some, struck down by fell disease
  Are breathing out their life;
And others, maimed by cruel wounds,
  Have left the deadly strife.

Ah, Marty! Marty, only think
  Of all the boys have done
And suffered in this weary war!
  Brave heroes, every one!
Oh! often, often in the night,
  I hear their voices call:
"*Come on and help us. Is it right
  That we should bear it all?*"

And when I kneel and try to pray,
  My thoughts are never free,
But cling to those who toil and fight
  And die for you and me.
And when I pray for victory,
  It seems almost a sin
To fold my hands and ask for what
  I will not help to win.

Oh! do not cling to me and cry,
  For it will break my heart;
I'm sure you'd rather have me die
  Than not to bear my part.
You think that some should stay at home
  To care for those away;
But still I'm helpless to decide
  If I should go or stay.

For, Marty, all the soldiers love,
  And all are loved again;
And I am loved, and love, perhaps,
  No more than other men.
I cannot tell—I do not know—
  Which way my duty lies,
Or where the Lord would have me build
  My fire of sacrifice.

I feel—I know—I am not mean;
  And, though I seem to boast,
I'm sure that I would give my life
  To those who need it most.

Perhaps the Spirit will reveal
  That which is fair and right;
So, Marty, let us humbly kneel
  And pray to Heaven for light.

Peace in the clover-scented air,
  And stars within the dome;
And underneath, in dim repose,
  A plain, New England home.
Within, a widow in her weeds,
  From whom all joy is flown,
Who kneels among her sleeping babes,
  And weeps and prays alone!

TO A SLEEPING SINGER.

LOVE in her heart, and song upon her lip—
A daughter, friend, and wife—
She lived a beauteous life,
And love and song shall bless her in her sleep.
The flowers whose language she interpreted,
The delicate airs, calm eves, and starry skies
That touched so sweetly her chaste sympathies,
And all the grieving souls she comforted,
Will bathe in separate sorrows the dear mound,
Where heart and harp lie silent and profound.
Oh, Woman! all the songs thou left to us
We will preserve for thee, in grateful love;
Give thou return of our affection thus,
And keep for us the songs thou sing'st above!

SONG AND SILENCE.

"My Mabel, you once had a bird
In your throat; and it sang all the day!
But now it sings never a word:
    Has the bird flown away?

"Oh sing to me, Mabel, again!
Strike the chords! Let the old fountain
        flow
With its balm for my fever and pain,
    As it did years ago!"

Mabel sighed (while a tear filled and fell,)
"I have bade all my singing adieu;
But I've a true story to tell,
    And I'll tell it to you.

"There's a bird's nest up there in the
oak,
On the bough that hangs over the stream,
And last night the mother-bird broke
Into song in her dream.

"This morning she woke, and was still;
For she thought of the frail little things
That needed her motherly bill,
Waiting under her wings.

"And busily, all the day long,
She hunted and carried their food,
And forgot both herself and her song
In her care for her brood.

"I sang in my dream, and you heard;
I woke, and you wonder I'm still;
But a mother is always a bird
With a fly in its bill!"

ALONE!

ALL alone in the world! all alone!
With a child on my knee, or a wife on
my breast,
Or, sitting beside me, the beautiful guest
Whom my heart leaps to greet as its sweet-
est and best,
Still alone in the world! all alone!

With my visions of beauty, alone!
Too fair to be painted, too fleet to be
scanned,
Too regal to stay at my feeble command,
They pass from the grasp of my impotent
hand:
Still alone in the world! all alone!

Alone with my conscience, alone!
Not an eye that can see when its finger of flame
Points my soul to its sin, or consumes it with shame!
Not an ear that can hear its low whisper of blame!
Still alone in the world! all alone!

In my visions of self, all alone!
The weakness, the meanness, the guilt that I see,
The fool or the fiend I am tempted to be,
Can only be seen and repented by me:
Still alone in the world! all alone!

Alone in my worship, alone!
No hand in the universe, joining with mine,
Can lift what it lays on the altar divine,
Or bear what it offers aloft to its shrine:
Still alone in the world! all alone!

In the valley of death, all alone!
The sighs and the tears of my friends are
in vain,
For mine is the passage, and mine is the
pain,
And mine the sad sinking of bosom and
brain:
Still alone in the world! all alone!

Not alone! never, never alone!
There is one who is with me by day and
by night,
Who sees and inspires all my visions of
light,
And teaches my conscience its office aright:
Not alone in the world! not alone!

Not alone! never, never alone!
He sees all my weakness with pitying eyes,
He helps me to lift my faint heart to the
skies,
And in my last passion he suffers and dies:
Not alone! never, never alone!

ALBERT DURER'S STUDIO.

In the house of Albert Durer
  Still is seen the studio
Where the pretty Nurembergers
  (Cheeks of rose and necks of snow)
Sat to have their portraits painted,
  Thrice a hundred years ago.

Still is seen the little loop-hole
  Where Frau Durer's jealous care
Watched the artist at his labor,
  And the sitter in her chair,
To observe each word and motion
  That should pass between the pair.

Handsome, hapless Albert Durer
  Was as circumspect and true

As the most correct of husbands,
  When the dear delightful shrew
Has him, and his sweet companions,
  Every moment under view.

But I trow that Albert Durer
  Had within his heart a spot
Where he sat, and painted pictures
That gave beauty to his lot,
And the sharp, intrusive vision
  Of Frau Durer entered not.

Ah! if brains and hearts had loop-holes,
  And Frau Durer could have seen
All the pictures that his fancy
  Hung upon their walls within,
How minute had been her watching,
  And how good he would have been!

THE OLD CLOCK OF PRAGUE.

THERE'S a curious clock in the city of
Prague—
A remarkable old astronomical clock—
With a dial whose outline is that of an
egg,
And with figures and fingers a wonder-
ful stock.

It announces the dawn and the death of
the day,
Shows the phases of moons and the
changes of tides,
Counts the months and the years as they
vanish away,
And performs quite a number of mar-
vels besides.

At the left of the dial a skeleton stands;
  And aloft hangs a musical bell in the tower,
Which he rings, by a rope that he holds in his hands,
  In his punctual function of striking the hour.

And the skeleton nods, as he tugs at the rope,
  At an odd little figure that eyes him aghast,
As a hint that the bell rings the knell of his hope,
  And the hour that is solemnly tolled is his last.

And the effigy turns its queer features away
  (Much as if for a snickering fit or a sneeze),
With a shrug and a shudder, that struggle to say:

"Pray excuse me, but—just an hour more,
if you please!"

But the funniest sight, of the numerous
sights
Which the clock has to show to the peo-
ple below,
Is the Holy Apostles in tunics and tights,
Who revolve in a ring, or proceed in a
row.

Their appearance can hardly be counted
sublime;
And their movements are formal, it must
be allowed;
But they're prompt, for they always appear
upon time,
And polite, for they bow very low to the
crowd.

This machine (so reliable papers record)
Was the work, from his own very clever design
Of one Hanusch, who died in the year of our Lord
One thousand four hundred and ninety and nine.

Did the people receive it with honor? you ask;
Did it bring a reward to the builder? Ah, well!
It was proper that they should have paid for the task!
And they did, in a way that it shocks me to tell.

For suspecting that Hanusch might grow to be vain,
Or that cities around them might covet their prize,

They invented a story that he was insane,
And, to stop him from labor, extinguished his eyes!

But the cunning old artist, though dying in shame,
May be sure that he labored and lived not amiss;
For his clock has outlasted the foes of his fame,
And the world owes him much for a lesson like this:

That a private success is a public offence,
That a citizen's fame is a city's disgrace,
And that both should be shunned by a person of sense,
Who would live with a whole pair of eyes in his face.

A CHRISTMAS CAROL.

THERE'S a song in the air!
There's a star in the sky!
There's a mother's deep prayer
And a baby's low cry!
And the star rains its fire while the Beau-
tiful sing,
For the manger of Bethlehem cradles a
king.

There's a tumult of joy
O'er the wonderful birth,
For the virgin's sweet boy
Is the Lord of the earth,
Ay! the star rains its fire and the Beau-
tiful sing,
For the manger of Bethlehem cradles a
king!

In the light of that star
Lie the ages impearled;
And that song from afar
Has swept over the world.
Every hearth is aflame, and the Beautiful sing
In the homes of the nations that Jesus is King.

We rejoice in the light,
And we echo the song
That comes down through the night
From the heavenly throng.
Ay! we shout to the lovely evangel they bring,
And we greet in his cradle our Saviour and King!

VERSES READ AT THE HADLEY CENTENNIAL.

(JUNE 9, 1859.)

HEART of Hadley, slowly beating
  Under midnight's azure breast,
Silence thy strong pulse repeating
  Wakes me—shakes me—from my rest.*

Hark! a beggar at the basement!
  Listen! friends are at the door!
There's a lover at the casement!
  There are feet upon the floor!

But they knock with muffled hammers,
  They step softly like the rain,
And repeat their gentle clamors
  Till I sleep and dream again.

* The pulsations of Hadley Falls, on the Connecticut, are felt for many miles around, in favorable conditions of the atmosphere.

Still the knocking at the basement;
  Still the rapping at the door;
Tireless lover at the casement;
  Ceaseless feet upon the floor.

Bolts are loosed by spectral fingers,
  Windows open through the gloom,
And the lilacs and syringas
  Breathe their perfume through the room.

'Mid the odorous pulsations
  Of the air around my bed,
Throng the ghostly generations
  Of the long forgotten dead.

"Rise and write!" with gentle pleading
  They command and I obey;
And I give to you the reading
  Of their tender words to-day.

"Children of the old plantation,
Heirs of all we won and held,
Greet us in your celebration—
Us—the nameless ones of Eld!

"We were never squires or teachers,
We were neither wise nor great,
But we listened to our preachers,
Worshipped God and loved the State.

"Blood of ours is on the meadow,
Dust of ours is in the soil,
But no marble casts a shadow
Where we slumber from our toil.

"Unremembered, unrecorded,
We are sleeping side by side,
And to names is now awarded
That for which the nameless died.

"We were men of humble station;
  We were women pure and true;
And we served our generation,—
  Lived and worked and fought for you.

"We were maidens, we were lovers,
  We were husbands, we were wives;
But oblivion's mantle covers
  All the sweetness of our lives."

"Praise the men who ruled and led us;
  Carry garlands to their graves;
But remember that your meadows
  Were not planted by their slaves.

"Children of the old plantation,
  Heirs of all we won and held,
Greet us in your celebration,—
  Us, the nameless ones of Eld."

This their message, and I send it,
  Faithful to their sweet behest,
And my toast shall e'en attend it,
  To be read among the rest.

Fill to all the brave and blameless
  Who, forgotten, passed away!
Drink the memory of the nameless,—
  Only named in heaven to-day!

WANTED.

GOD give us men! A time like this demands
Strong minds, great hearts, true faith, and ready hands;
Men whom the lust of office does not kill;
  Men whom the spoils of office cannot buy;
Men who possess opinions and a will;
  Men who have honor,—men who will not lie;
Men who can stand before a demagogue,
  And damn his treacherous flatteries without winking!
Tall men, sun-crowned, who live above the fog
  In public duty, and in private thinking:
For while the rabble, with their thumb-worn creeds,

Their large professions and their little
deeds,—
Mingle in selfish strife, lo! Freedom weeps,
Wrong rules the land, and waiting Justice
sleeps!

MERLE THE COUNSELLOR.

OLD MERLE, the counsellor and guide,
And tall young Rolfe walked side by side
At the sweet hour of eventide.

The yellow light of parting day
Upon the peaceful landscape lay,
And touched the mountain far away.

The tinkling of the distant herds,
And the low twitter of the birds
Mingled with childhood's happy words.

The old man raised his trembling palm,
And bared his brow to meet the balm
That fell with twilight's dewy calm;

And one could see that to his thought,
The scenes and sounds around him brought
Suggestions of the heaven he sought.

But Rolfe, his young companion, bent
His moody brow in discontent,
And sadly murmured as he went.

For vagrant passions, fierce and grim,
And fearful memories haunted him,
That made the evening glory dim.

Then spoke the cheerful voice of Merle:
"Where yonder clouds their gold unfurl,
One almost sees the gates of pearl.

"Nay, one can hardly look amiss
For heaven, in such a scene as this,
Or fail to feel its present bliss.

"So near we stand to holy things,
And all our high imaginings,
That faith forgets to lift her wings!"

Then answered Rolfe, with bitter tone:
"If thou hast visions of the throne,
Enjoy them; they are all thy own.

"For me there lives no God of love;
For me there bends no heaven above;
And Peace, the gently brooding dove,

"Has flown afar, and in her stead
Fierce vultures wheel above my head,
And hope is sick and faith is dead.

"Death can but loose a loathsome bond,
And from the depths of my despond,
I see no ray of light beyond."

It was a sad, discordant strain,
That brought old Merle to earth again,
And filled his soul with solemn pain.

At length they reached a leafy wood,
And walked in silence, till they stood
Within the fragrant solitude.

Then spake old Merle with gentle art:
"I know the secret of thy heart,
And will, if thou desire, impart."

Rolfe answered with a hopeless sigh,
But from the tear that brimmed his eye,
The old man gladly caught reply,

And spoke: "Beyond these forest trees
A city stands; and sparkling seas
Waft up to it the evening breeze.

"Thou canst not see its gilded domes,
Its plume of smoke, its pleasant homes,
Or catch the gleam of surf that foams

"And dies upon its verdant shore,
But there it stands; and there the roar
Of life shall swell for evermore!

"The path we walk is fair and wide,
But still our vision is denied
The city and its nursing tide.

"The path we walk is wide and fair,
But curves and wanders here and there,
And builds the wall of our despair.

"Make straight the path, and then shall
shine
Through trembling walls of tree and vine
The vision fair for which we pine.

"And thou, my son, so long hast been
Along the crooked ways of sin,
That they have closed, and shut thee in.

"Make straight the path before thy feet,
And walk within it firm and fleet,
And thou shalt see, in vision sweet

"And constant as the love supreme,
With closer gaze and brighter beam,
The peaceful heaven that fills my dream."

He paused: no more his lips could say;
And then, beneath the twilight gray,
The silent pair retraced their way.

But in the young man's eyes a light
Shone strong and resolute and bright,
For which Merle thanked his God that night.

DANIEL GRAY.

If I shall ever win the home in heaven
For whose sweet rest I humbly hope and pray,
In the great company of the forgiven
I shall be sure to find old Daniel Gray.

I knew him well; in truth, few knew him better;
For my young eyes oft read for him the Word,
And saw how meekly from the crystal letter
He drank the life of his beloved Lord.

Old Daniel Gray was not a man who lifted
On ready words his freight of gratitude,
Nor was he called among the gifted,
In the prayer-meetings of his neighborhood.

He had a few old-fashioned words and
phrases,
Linked in with sacred texts and Sunday
rhymes;
And I suppose that in his prayers and graces,
I've heard them all at least a thousand times.

I see him now—his form, his face, his motions,
His homespun habit, and his silver hair,—
And hear the language of his trite devotions,
Rising behind the straight-backed kitchen
chair.

I can remember how the sentence sounded—
"Help us, O Lord, to pray and not to
faint!"
And how the "conquering-and-to conquer"
rounded
The loftier aspirations of the saint.

He had some notions that did not improve
him,
He never kissed his children—so they
say;
And finest scenes and fairest flowers would
move him
Less than a horse-shoe picked up in the
way.

He had a hearty hatred of oppression,
And righteous words for sin of every kind;
Alas, that the transgressor and transgres-
sion
Were linked so closely in his honest mind!

He could see nought but vanity in beauty,
And naught but weakness in a fond caress,
And pitied men whose views of Christian
duty
Allowed indulgence in such foolishness.

Yet there were love and tenderness within
him;
And I am told that when his Charley
died,
Nor nature's need nor gentle words could
win him
From his fond vigils at the sleeper's side.

And when they came to bury little Charlie,
They found fresh dew-drops sprinkled in his
hair,
And on his breast a rose-bud gathered
early,
And guessed, but did not know who placed
it there.

Honest and faithful, constant in his calling,
Strictly attendant on the means of grace,
Instant in prayer, and fearful most of fall-
ing,
Old Daniel Gray was always in his place.

A practical old man, and yet a dreamer,
He thought that in some strange, unlooked-
for way
His mighty Friend in Heaven, the great
Redeemer,
Would honor him with wealth some golden
day.

This dream he carried in a hopeful spirit
Until in death his patient eye grew dim,
And his Redeemer called him to inherit
The heaven of wealth long garnered up for
him.

So, if I ever win the home in heaven
For whose sweet rest I humbly hope and
pray,
In the great company of the forgiven
I shall be sure to find old Daniel Gray.

THE MOUNTAIN CHRISTENING.

(A Legend of The Connecticut.)

HOW did they manage to busy themselves—
  Our sires, in the early plantation days?
Grinding their axes and whittling their
    helves?
  Fishing for salmon and planting maize?

How when the chopping and splitting were
    done?
  How when the corn-fields were planted and
    hoed?
How when the salmon had ceased to run,
  And the bushes were cleared from the old
    Bay Road?

They were not men who stood still in their
shoes,
Or who clung to their cabins when forests
were damp;
So, when labor was finished, they cut the
blues
And their sticks for a lively exploring
tramp.

'Twas a beautiful morning in June, they
say—
Two hundred and twenty years ago,
When armed and equipped for a holiday,
They stood where Connecticut's waters
flow,

With five upon this side and five upon
that,—
Agawam's bravest and hardiest men,
Hailing each other with lusty chat,
That the tall woods caught and tossed
over again.

Holyoke, the gentle and daring, stood
  On the Eastern bank with his trusty four,
And Rowland Thomas, the gallant and good,
  Headed the band on the other shore.

"Due North!" shouted Holyoke and all his men.
  "Due North!" answered they on the opposite beach;
And northward they started, the sturdy ten,
  With their haversacks filled and a musket each.

The women ran panting to bid them good-bye
  And sweet Mary Pynchon was there (I guess),
With a sigh in her throat and a tear in her eye
  As Holyoke marched into the wilderness,

And the boys were all wondering where
they would go,
And what they would meet in the dangerous way;
And the good wives were gossiping to and
fro,
And prating and shaking their heads all
day

Up the bright river they travelled abreast,
Calling each other from bank to bank,
Till the hot sun slowly rolled into the West,
And gilded the mountain-tops where it sank.

They lighted their camp-fires and ate of their
fare,
And drank of the water that ran at their
feet,
And wrapped in the balm of the cool evening
air,
Sank down to a sleep that was dreamless
and sweet.

The great falls roared in their ears all night,
And the sturgeon splashed and the wild-cat screamed,
But they did not wake till the morning light
Red through the willowy branches beamed.

Brief was the toilet and short the grace,
And strong were the viands that broke their fast;
Then onward they pressed till they reached the place
Where the river between two mountains passed.

Up the rough ledges they clambered amain,
Holyoke and Thomas on either hand,
Till high in mid-passage they paused, and then
They tearfully gazed on a lovely land.

Down by the Ox-Bow's southerly shore
  Licking the wave bowed an antlered buck;
And Northward and Westward a league or
      more
  Stretched the broad meadows of Nono-
      tuck.

Straight up the river an Indian town
  Filled the soft air with its musical hum,
And children's voices were wafted down
  From the peaceful shadows of Hockanum.

Rude little patches of greening maize
  Dappled the landscape far and wide,
And away in the North in the sunset's blaze,
  Sugar-loaf stood and was glorified!

The morning dawned on the double group
  Facing each other on opposite shores,
Where ages ago with a mighty swoop
  The waters parted the mountain doors.

"Let us christen the mountains," said Holyoke in glee;
"Let us christen the mountains," said Thomas again;
"That mountain for you, and this mountain for me!"
And their trusty fellows responded: "Amen!"

Then Holyoke buried his palm in the stream,
And tossed the pure spray toward the mountain's brow,
And said, while it shone in the sun's first beam,
"Fair mountain, thou art Mount Holyoke now!"

The sun shone full on the Western height,
When Thomas came up from the crystal tide:

"I name thee Thomas by Christian rite!"
  "Thou art Mount Thomas!" they all replied.

They paused but a moment when rounding a bluff
  Shot an Indian's boat with its stealthy oar,
And with strings of wampum and gaudy stuff
  They beckoned it in to the Western shore.

Gracious and brief was the bargain made
  By the white man's potent pantomime;
And the delicate boat with its dainty blade
  Bore them over the river one man at a time.

There were greetings and jests in every mouth,
  And hearty farewells to "Holyoke" and "Tom":

Then the gleeful men turned their steps due
South,
And took a bee-line for Agawam.

They passed Willimansett at noon that day,
And Chicopee just as the sun went down,
And when the last daylight had faded away,
All hungry and weary they entered the
town.

Mr. Pynchon demanded a full report,
Which Holyoke wrote for the two com-
mands;
And when he went down to the General
Court
He placed it in Governor Winthrop's
hands.

A GOLDEN WEDDING-SONG.

THE links of fifty golden years
  Reach to the golden ring
Which now, with glad and grateful tears,
  We celebrate and sing.
O chain of love! O ring of gold!
  That have the years defied;
And still in happy bondage hold
  The old man and his bride!

The locks are white that once were black;
  The sight is feebler grown;
But through the long and weary track
  The heart has held its own!
O chain of love! O ring of gold!
  That time could not divide;
That kept through changes manifold
  The old man with his bride!

The little ones have come and gone;
  The old have passed away;
But love—immortal love—lives on,
  And blossoms 'mid decay.
O chain of love! O ring of gold!
  That have the years defied;
And still with growing strength infold
  The old man and his bride!

The golden bridal! ah, how sweet
  The music of its bell,
To those whose hearts the vows repeat
  Their lives have kept so well!
O chain of love! O ring of gold!
  O marriage true and tried!
That bind with tenderness untold
  The old man to his bride!

www.ingramcontent.com/pod-product-compliance
Lightning Source LLC
LaVergne TN
LVHW021424110826
845150LV00007B/2072

* 9 7 8 1 4 2 5 5 0 9 0 5 7 *